I0532264

STEPS OF GRACE

Ladder of Mercy

Natasha R.
McCoy

STEPS OF GRACE
Ladder of Mercy

Copyright © 2023 by Natasha R. McCoy

Hair stylist: Tara Ramcharan, rtrsav@yahoo.com
Photographer: Simon Pierre, hiddensecretphotography@gmail.com
Makeup artist: Kenya Downing, kenyaenhancingbeauty.com

RHG Media Productions
25495 Southwick Drive #103
Hayward, CA 94544.

Changing Names & Medical Advice
Some names and identifying details have been changed to protect the
privacy of individuals. This book is not intended as a substitute for the
medical advice of physicians. The reader should regularly consult a
physician in matters relating to his/her health and particularly with respect
to any symptoms that may require diagnosis or medical attention.

All rights reserved. No part of this publication may be reproduced
distributed or transmitted in any form or by any means including
photocopying recording or other electronic or mechanical means
without proper written permission of author or publisher, except
in the case of brief quotations embodied in critical reviews and
certain other noncommercial uses permitted by copyright law.

ISBN 979-8-9884342-0-7 (paperback)
ISBN 979-8-9884342-1-4 (hardcover)

Visit us on line at www.YourPurposeDrivenPractice.com
Printed in the United States of America.

What People Are Saying

"This riveting book will have you turning pages quickly as Natasha takes you through her experiences and that of other abuse survivors. "
—Dr. Elizabeth Clamon

"As a fellow child sexual abuse survivor, reading her words about encouragement and perseverance lifted me up and helped me know that I am not alone in my journey. "
—Tracy Kelly

"The author expresses that a relationship with God is essential, with friends and a support group can lead to freedom, self-acceptance and love. A must-read book. "
—Toni Bruce, CEO, Motivational speaker, Best Selling Author
Precious Stones 4 Life LLC

"Steps of Grace, Ladder of Mercy is a powerful message of God's love for His Children whom He created. I recommend adding this book to your reading room. "
—Barry Bonner, Senior Pastor

"*Natasha's book led me to experience God's joy through His love, and longing for all of us to reach out, take hold of His hand and let Him guide us through to a brighter tomorrow. I believe there are better days that await us. What beautiful lessons and stories were shared in this book!*"

—Deborah Wiener

"*Her desire to tell her story is motivated in the spirit of helping other adults who have experienced trauma as a child by opening up about her experience. Anyone facing similar history may find this book a worthwhile component to surviving and thriving as they heal from trauma.*"

—JoEllen Revell, LCSW
Program Director, Victim Service Center of Central Florida

"*The trauma of childhood sexual abuse, the courage to fight and the power of one woman to heal.*"

—Maureen Ryan Blake
Maureen Ryan Blake Media Productions

Contents

Foreword

BY DENISE E. GREAVES, EDD, JD, EDS, MBA/HRM

et off me!!! You're inside me!!

G I remember that night as if it were yesterday. I was taking a shortcut through the park on my way to the bus station from my high school sports day. He came from behind and grabbed me, punched me in the face, and split my lip. I still have the scar on my lower right lip reminding me of that awful night. I remember the smell on his breath, that smell of drugs and cigarettes. I smelt him for years after he forced himself inside me.

There is something powerful about hearing the words of another survivor of sexual offense, another person who has been there with you. You may ask why I use the word *survivor*. After a few years of struggling and trying to cope with this traumatic experience, I was adamant not to become a victim. This experience haunted me for years, even into my marriage. During intercourse with my husband, I would often go into a crisis and fight with my husband as if I were fighting with my rapist. I could smell my rapist as my husband was on top of me. It took many sessions of therapy in order to overcome this and have a normal sexual relationship.

People who hear about the experience of the survivor of rape will naturally offer words of support or encouragement. Your brothers and sisters in faith will tell you: just

pray about it; with prayer and faith, you will receive healing; you need to trust the Lord more. When these words
come from persons who have not experienced the trauma
of rape, they lack credibility and mean absolutely nothing
to the survivor of rape. You see, the body of the survivor
of rape keeps score of the traumatic rape experience.
Natasha's memoir walks us through her struggles with guilt
and feelings of insignificance over the years. Only another
survivor of sexual assault can truly understand the powers
of the mind and body and its impact on the body years
after surviving being violated.

I met Natasha over ten years ago and was immediately
drawn to her. We connected immediately, and the relationship grew quickly. Over the years, I learned of her struggles
to cope with the memories of the molestation. I saw her
display of strength even when she was in emotional turmoil. We talked about the repeated accounts she experienced as a child and her struggles with the memories and
guilt into adulthood. I remember us having a discussion
about this and the likelihood that her sometimes defen-
siveness and seeming aggression could be a result of this
experience. I remember talking to Natasha about speaking
with a professional who could give her ideas to cope with
the emotions she sometimes experienced as a result of the
abuse. Speaking to a professional worked for me, and I
was confident it would work for her. Natasha, like myself
and other survivors of sexual trauma, are human beings
struggling to repair our lives. You see, rape's power can
make you feel severed from the rest of life.

As you read *Steps of Grace, Ladder of Mercy*, you will find
this book to be a collection of Natasha's deepest pains.
However, we will not just read of her pains but will also

get to travel through this journey towards recovery and her relationship with and dependence on God. Every single chapter of this book was handwritten by this woman I know personally and call a friend. As you read each chapter, you will see how Natasha spends each day trying to heal a bit more. When a survivor of assault speaks of their inner strength and feeling of empowerment and says *God is not finished with me yet,* these are not mere platitudes or slogans. These words expressed by this brave and strong author have been forged in a crucible of scorching turmoil; believe me, I have been there. The right for Natasha to say these words has been earned.

This book is for survivors of rape who are in turmoil, who feel as though life is not worth living and struggle with whether they should live or die. This book is for survivors who feel as though they are being smothered by this extreme ordeal and cannot see that light at the end of the tunnel. This book is for the young lady who hides the mark on her body from a brutal assault. This book is for the woman whose husband or boyfriend has lost patience with her because "it happened years ago; you should be over it." This book is for the woman who is in therapy and is wondering if therapy is working or whether she is so messed up that therapy will never work. This book is for the survivor of rape who knows there are other survivors of rape yet still sees herself as a victim.

Acknowledgments

I would like to extend my deepest gratitude to my phenomenal editor, Doreen Priscilla Brown, for her dazzling ability and keen mind, along with her expression of compassion.

To my children Danielle and Allan Sexius for encouraging, supporting, and saying how proud you are of my endeavors. I appreciate your honesty. Even when I make you frustrated, you are understanding. You guys motivate me.

To my husband, Deryck, for always verbalizing how God's transforming power continues to work through forgiveness.

To my niece Arveon, who skillfully and precisely captured my vision of the book cover, described via phone conversation. Your talent is truly from God. I love you.

To my dear friend Denise Greaves, thanks for the many times of laughter, for your wisdom and kindness, and also for trusting me with your vulnerability over the years. What a powerful foreword; my gratitude is unbounded. You are so precious to me.

To my beloved friend and prayer partner, Brenda Hunt, who listened to me vent and cry, yet reminded me of my strength and blessings in the lives of others and eagerly anticipated the completion of this book.

To my childhood best friend, Abigail Mercury, I am extremely grateful for the many years of support. Your daily spiritual upliftment helps me to stay anchored in Christ. My sincere thanks for holding me accountable for writing weekly towards this task and for saying, "That's awesome, Tash," when I did. My deepest appreciation for loving me with all my flaws.

To my counselor, Maryann Haselden, for prompting me to dictate my experiences, thoughts and feelings for our weekly meetings.

To Pastor Alex Williams, I extend special thanks for your encouragement to pursue publishing in order to help others know of God's amazing Grace. And yes, Pastor Mark Brown, for being a man of your word and connecting me to the amazing "Professor." For that I am indebted.

The Journey

T his memoir is a clarion call to women and men who battle feelings of "never good enough."

When you first meet me in these pages, I am still struggling with bouts of guilt and insignificance.

I see you.

I greet you.

I flash spurts of warmth in your direction, yet I do not show you all that is me! The truth is this: I am covering my true feelings.

I am hiding behind a cloud of dust, feeling that, upon meeting me, you will somehow be exposed to my flaws.

And if you are introduced to my imperfection, my greatest fear is that you will judge me.

So I asked myself the question: How do I arrive at the point where I no longer see my flaws as fatal, but merely as wounds that my Creator so badly wants to turn into miracles?

Like someone so aptly put it: "You don't have to broadcast your trauma to the world, yet your trauma should be exposed if only as a testimony to help someone who might be sitting on the edge of a proverbial cliff, waiting to be pulled back into reality."

I mentioned the word *trauma,* and even as I did, that word caused anxiety. Ironically, the more I tried to erase it from my memory, the larger it became.

Trauma! It's not a one-size-fits-all. Because each individual has different coping skills, so likewise each person's ability to cope with the aftermath of sexual trauma differs.

There are so many reasons for this disparity, but even under the most "ideal" of circumstances, sexual trauma rips open the soul; it leaves lasting wounds; and, sometimes, sexual trauma causes extinction.

I am zeroing in on my recollection of where my trauma found me! It happened at the tender age of five, when all I wanted to be was a kid playing hopscotch and dipping my feet in roadside mud puddles; but little did I realize that there were sexual abusers lurking, right in my backyard.

Perhaps that is what compounds my hurt.

Did no one see this coming?

Could even I have done something to prevent these individuals from stripping me of my innocence?

These are no longer childhood musings, for even decades later these questions run askew in my mind, haunting me, gnawing at my memory.

And those feelings of shame—gross shame? Sometimes they come in patches—patches of anger trading places with sadness, longing for sunlight.

I once heard a story about a famous athlete who, at the height of his career, was struggling with the decision to come out of the closet. As the story goes, he struggled for years, devising a five-point plan for breaking the news. He imagined the world so large, yet his world so small—small enough that every person he would meet would know he was an impostor. This is exactly how he was expressing himself!

My challenge was much the same. I imagined myself living in a particular body one day, then suddenly transitioning into a different body the next day. I was stopping and starting, stripped of all that was and trying to squeeze into what must now be.

I stood a step away from my mirror, still looking for clarity; but what did I see? Certainly not a beautiful woman who was smart and engaging, ready to take on the world! What a disappointment!

I am scared now—real scared! My larger world was my blood family I've known from birth, and my new world? As I am beginning to confront the inevitable, all I can see is a ball of confusion—a world littered with hostility and condemnation.

How dare I choose such a time to exhale? And if I did, would I lose my larger world to an unknown one?

"For I know the plans I have for you, said the Lord, plans to prosper you and to give you a future." (Jeremiah 29:11)

A moment of truth: If anyone tells you that you are stronger than you think you are, believe them! For before every mountaintop, there is a valley; and it is in those valleys that prayers are prayed and faith is strengthened. And even though the way forward may not always be clear, in fact it might even be obscured with thorns and thistles, it is good enough to believe that God, the miraculous way-maker will make a way.

I believe that inherent in all of us is an innate and compelling ability to cope. We might throw around terms like *deflection, distractions, coping mechanisms,* and sometimes *denial,* but we all have them, built in. To show you an example of how it works: During my low moments when I needed time away from my hurtful memories, I found solace in play time at home and at school. The more I played, the happier I became, and the happier I became, the more I felt like a child without a care in the world. How I wished play time would last forever! To my chagrin, it did not!

On the journey, there were times that taking my life—suicide—actually crossed my mind on more than one occasion. And even though I did not fully grasp the volatility of the word *suicide* at that tender age, I knew that it was a "forever and done" situation. I contemplated: Why not? Why stay? I wavered. Did it matter whether I existed or ceased to exist?

The pulling and hauling, tugging, and pulling back, as I recall them, were continuing well after the knives and other sharp objects were introduced into my "forever and done" plan. Somehow, as hard as I pressed, the force I used was counteracted by a stronger one pulling away.

Sometimes mysteries are just that, mysteries, and what better place to go for confirmation than to the story of Abraham in Genesis 22:6, where Abraham is directed by God to offer up his son Isaac as a sacrifice.

As I read, purposefully, I literally froze at the point where Abraham had already raised the knife and stretched out his hand to apply the fatal blow to his son lying on the altar. Something mysterious happened. It was as if the act in real time had become an act put on hold, for in my mind God was saying, "Hold it! I'm still writing the story, and I'm nowhere close to the concluding chapter!"

I rushed to my bedroom, bawling, and I cried out to God. "This is my story!" I wept, and wept, and wept some more.

What an interactive up-close and personal moment between God and Abraham, where faith and obedience met in the center of the activity! And this part gripped me more than any other: Abraham obeyed, even without knowing that God had already made provisions to accomplish the act.

Was this God's way of using Abraham's story to help me navigate my own ordeal? Was this God's way of confirming his plans to prosper me with a beautiful future, as promised in Jeremiah 29:11? Were all these things getting into formation as part of the bigger picture?

Lying in a dark room, mentally communicating with God, I asked: *What is it about me that I wasn't allowed to succeed at committing suicide while others achieve their goal?* His audible response was, "Mercy Said No." Tears flowed, seeming endless. Squeezing my eyes tightly, I bit softly on my upper lip, attempting to contain my emotion. That was not the commitment he desired for me, but rather a subjection of myself and the issues to him, the only one who is all-powerful, consuming me with his spirit to enable me to cope whenever the unwelcome memories stir up pain and sadness.

Look, the God who knew me before I was formed in my mother's womb also understood the flaws in my contemplation of executing my "forever and done" plan. And the fact that he used his divine hands to retard the sharp object from searing through my veins was undoubtedly his way of preserving my life, not only to eventually inherit his kingdom to come, but to help me comfort others in their journey of pain.

I have been questioning myself as to why sexual abuse has seemingly been on the front burner in recent years. How prevalent were these acts in the past? Why do they seem so pervasive in recent history? So I want you to fly over with me to help the answer along. One answer, among others, could be that technology and social media have together created watershed moments for perfect-storm stories, and that, together, these have brought about a sense of empowerment to the voiceless. And, as always is the case whenever light appears, the entire room lights up, and that light exposes all the secrets. I guess that if we first understand that the crime of rape is nothing new, it is important for victims or survivors to understand that it is the perpetrators and not the survivor who bear responsibility for this horrific crime. For even as I defer to scriptures, it is not lost on me that the Bible is replete with accounts of rapes and other cases of sexual abuse and their devastating effects on families and nations.

In Genesis 34:1-2, Dinah was raped by Shechem. Judges 19:22–29 gives an account of a host who volunteered to throw the female occupant out of his household into the street, where a gang of men were waiting "for the strike." On that occasion, the concubine of the host was gang-raped, killed, and mutilated. These are the results of the stony hearts of mankind being unlike the loving kindness God expects us to have for one another.

I had been making random notes here and there for some time, but it wasn't until I summoned the courage to take all the little bits and pieces, journal and all, that I began the process of writing a real book. Oddly enough, 2022 was one of the most eventful years I can remember, at least for women.

For me, reflecting and becoming more aware of women's achievements both past and present was viewed as empowerment where anything and everything was possible. Mae Jemison was the first African-American woman in space. Michelle Obama was the United States' first African-American first lady. Janet Reno was our first female attorney general. Meghan Markle married into the British royal family. Dorothy Vaughan was NASA's first African-American manager. Madeleine Albright was our first female secretary of state. Kamala Harris is our first African-American vice president. Amanda Gorman is a young African-American woman who wrote and read her poem at the 2020 US presidential inauguration. Those events are not named in any particular order, and many other women "firsts" preceded them and are greatly admired. I stated the women mentioned as first in accomplishment because they are recorded as such in history; however, rank is irrelevant. Set no limits on what you want to achieve, and get it done.

There is something empowering about observing women, particularly women of color, breaking the glass ceiling and venturing far beyond what they themselves could hardly imagine! For my part, as time rolled on and glass ceilings were shattered and roles were reversed, surpassed, or equaled, I found strength in the knowledge that I, too, can ignore at least some of the chains that had me weighed down. I realized that I can talk to the world, up close and personal, through written pages. Thus, in faith, *Steps of Grace, Ladder of Mercy* was birthed, and this is my story—this is my song.

I hope in sharing my story, I can show you that you are not alone and you can have hope, healing, and a powerful and an empowering future! You matter and are beautifully and wonderfully made. You can heal, rise up, and live fully, deeply, and in an empowered way.

CHAPTER 1

Living in Anger: Hell on Earth

Triggers, oh triggers!

When your therapist tells you to "own your anger" or something like that, it's not mixed messaging. It is helpful! What it does not mean is that you make anger yours. It does mean, however, that anger is a normal part of "your" healing process. I had to learn that!

A huge challenge: People around you may not quite understand your outbursts, eruptions, silence, or even your mood swings. And they may even be quick to dismiss you or label you as mean, evil, or even bipolar. Don't condemn them. Understand their dilemma—they have been thrust into an environment which they don't know how to cope with. That's where a good therapist comes in, but they don't have a magic bullet, either; however, they are trained in how to help you "manage" your anger.

Flashbacks and anger—one is the parent of the other.

The question *why me* seems to be my biggest Achilles' heel. Not that I wish my ordeal on anyone else, but why, why, why, why? Why me? But the search for an answer often lands right in the perpetrator's lap. That's progress!

I'm reliving my nightmare as I write.

Sporadic bouts of the most disgusting kind assail my mental space. The abuser's pungent odor! Imagery of his violent acts! Lying asleep on my side, only to feel someone pressing against me! Asleep on my stomach, awakened to a hand making its way to my crotch!

There came a numbness as I heard myself screaming uncontrollably, sounding the alarm to be rescued—but in the end it was a full-blown nightmare!

But so much of my ordeal was far from nightmarish! There were also times when I was left in the care of an older half brother, and just as he thought the coast was clear he demanded that I undress.

The plot continues! A neighbor's son would ask permission of my parent for me to accompany him to the store.

Store?

This was no store visit! It was all a clever scheme to lure me into thick bushes for sexual pleasure.

There are obvious gaps in some of the details because I am still choosing to skip the "goriness."

Another one of my troublesome "why" questions— why weren't reports made? I felt I did! Each incident was reported, though not clearly verbalized—I just didn't know how to.

Where am I today?

Deep are the scars from yesterday. Sometimes I feel like I am rebounding, other times not so much! For just when I believe all is well, I find myself the originator of bombastic outbursts whenever a situation seems to be going horribly wrong.

And if I told you I have serious trust issues in my personal relationships, believe me! Sometimes it feels like transitioning in an instant from Dr. Jekyll to Mr. Hyde.

Yet I press on, for, to quote an old adage: "God is not finished with me yet."

If you could look with me into my little space, you would immediately sense that through all my dog days of anguish, there was waving in front of me a pair of divine hands directing traffic. And even when I had considered veering off the correct path or worse, those hands guided me back with a "stay in your lane" command. Therefore, for as long as I live, I will trust God for his beautiful promises in Psalm 23. For now, I know that I can trust him with my journey as I sojourn through life's valley and shadow of death—

- I shall not want.

- God provides abundant green shrubbery for my soul.

- And even when my soul is crushed and broken, he does a masterful job at repairing it.

- He snatches me out of the hands of the evil one and sets my feet on the path of righteousness.

- And just when I think there is no more grace and mercy to claim, God tells me that he will not only provide enough for one episode in my life but will lather my soul with his abundant suds forever, even as I dwell with him in his forever space—all because he is my wonderful Shepherd whose storehouse is a relentless overflow of good things. A refreshing reminder in Psalms 84:11 reads, "For the Lord God is a sun and shield; The Lord will give grace and glory; No good thing will He withhold from those who walk uprightly."

CHAPTER 2

Wall of Defense

You've heard it! "Tall fences [walls] make good neighbors."

But no one ever talks about the back story about tall fences. The fact is that they provide nice privacy, and, for those who are introverts, anyway, they shield you from face-to-face contact with strangers.

But the conversation doesn't stop there. The tall fence does something else! It obscures your neighbor's view of your space to the point that if you are lying in your backyard rolling from side to side, struggling for air because an intruder has just knocked the wind out of you, no one could come and rescue you, not even as much as dial 911.

Such was the wall of defense I had erected in my life. It's not that every adult person who crossed my path was ill-intentioned; I have a hunch some were great people. But my past was in charge of my current situation, and I needed to block everyone out of my space.

Some introspection: as a professional now, having to deal with clients who confide in me, I understand more fully the nature of that beast that I had been dealing with—that deep-seated suspicion they have that danger is lurking and they have to protect all their unpalatable secrets.

That is the thousand-pound elephant in the room—distrust! And that is a lonely world! After all, who wants to be on stage with someone in your cast of characters who is afraid to as much as turn his back for a head shot?

Was that example more difficult than hanging with someone at a church social who thinks that every little comment or bit of small talk is designed as a put-down?

But even in my lonely world of self-absorption, there was that special childhood friend who accepted and liked me even when I disliked myself. We played and talked about things that brought on girlish laughter; how pain-relieving that was for me.

When we first met, we were kids in bows and bobby socks; now we are all grown up. But the fallout from an ugly childhood past never grows up; and even after all had been forgiven of the perpetrators and I moved on with a successful family and career, the scars from the shrapnel lingered.

But trust is a daily struggle—it is a universal struggle! And it is made even more complicated when your abuser is a family member or a friend. That builds your wall even higher!

Can You Put a Face on the Perpetrator?

I searched high and low trying to find a profile for the sexual abuser, and nowhere could I find a template. No one, even in anecdotal stories, was able to say that the sexual abuser exhibits a specific profile, is a certain height or of a certain color, has an educational level of a certain standard, is an islander or from the city—none of that! Perpetrators of the crime seem to transcend race, color, socioeconomic status, culture, even religion. And neither can you pin down the perpetrator's origin.

It might upset you to know that it's not just the neighbor or the coach that's eyeballing your youngster, but it could be a pastor, a dad, an uncle, or a brother, as victims in this book know firsthand in some cases. Included are popes, church leaders, trusted authority figures, family physicians, your divorce attorney, your bank manager, your manicurist, or even your child's classroom teacher. Sexual abuse is difficult to predict. Empower children with the courage to speak up at the first sign of abuse. Talk with your children early. Spare no scenario. Tell them about stranger-danger, but also tell them what to do about inappropriate touching by friends and family members. Give them an action plan. Everyone from parents to churches, schools, and youth clubs bears responsibility to arm youngsters with the tools necessary to make decisions about their bodies at an early age. Today's youngsters are introduced to salacious, seductive, harmful images and texts that do more than just mess up the minds of young girls; and boys are not excluded. They imprint on their tender minds the notion of valueless souls. And what happens when young girls fail to view their bodies as sacred and off limits? Let us equip our little ones so that they can grow having one less ordeal to combat.

Mothers who don't know

Some mothers don't just miss little signs, they miss red flags waving hysterically at them. Do they turn a blind eye? So much of life is a vicious cycle—what if the mother herself suffered a similar early-years fate, induced into "womanhood" by her own father or other family members? What if the mother is dependent on her young daughter's molester for economic sustenance, and to "rub him the wrong way" might mean discontinuation of economic aid? The what-ifs are numerous, and statistics don't even begin to tell the stories. Sometimes the anecdotal accounts are so much more powerful. Where to go for these stories? Talk to a high-school teacher or guidance counselor, and they will tell you about teenage girls who cry hysterically on their shoulders. Only as they get older do they begin to understand the extent of their quandary. Take a drive into some neighborhoods where homegrown once-upon-a-time stories of growing up in Sodom are freely shared. Here is what you will discover:

Child sexual abusers are usually charming. They are generous. They are affectionate. They are the neighbors you dream of having. They are great salesmen, and that's exactly how they get close to families they target—they ingratiate themselves into the family unit and become one of them. "So, Ted would never do such a thing," one mother defiantly said to her nine-year-old daughter, "and you should quit lying on him!" May God grant us wisdom to see beyond our assumptions to the signs that should be obvious.

Here are some suggestions to help protect your children and family:

1. *Know who you are bringing into your house.*

2. *Know where your youngsters are at all times.*

3. *Teach your children about signs to watch for.*

4. *Watch out for these boyfriends' roving eyes.*

5. *Don't grow up your children too fast. Let them understand their bodies.*

6. *Most of all, create a safe and loving home with open communication. If your children share with you something that scares them or makes them uncomfortable, listen to them and believe them.*

Why?

In writing this book, I am still struggling to figure out answers to questions such as: Why so much depravity? Why? Eve entertained and was inveigled by Satan, the originator of sin who then entered into the hearts of men, attacking God's moral laws for lustful desires. As earthly parents saw their offspring going awry, God's heart grieved that he had made man, because his word is clear about his initial plans for his children to embody his character. The enemy intercepted, and thereby death entered—not mere physical death, but also a decay in human social relations, familial relationships, spirituality, emotion, and the like. We have all fallen prey to the devil's snares.

In the meantime, it behooves everyone to show kindness to even the most difficult people. For if there is one thing all my readers could draw from the narratives in this book, it is this: because you may never know what secret demons or crucibles people are wrestling with, the general approach should be one of empathy rather than rebuke.

And who needs to remember this? A guidance counselor I ran across in my quest to find conversation on sexual abuse summed it up in this short prayer: "Father, I thank you for the gift of compassion. Help us to understand that our ability to show empathy is a reflection of the compassion you have for us. So, with this in mind, give us the grace to temper judgment with consideration. Take away the harshness from our souls and fill the void with a calm demeanor of grace and mercy. Amen."

29

CHAPTER 3

Sexually Abused Victims/Survivors Speak Out

I am still flashing back to my own story, and as I do, I can recount the times when all I needed was for some kind person to whisper in my ear: "You are of great worth because your Heavenly Father says you are the apple of his eye."

The raw truth is that victims of sexual abuse do not walk around with a tag on their chest that reads, "I've been sexually abused." However, I have found that they do walk around with a tag plastered on their souls that reads, "I've been sexually abused, and everybody knows I'm nothing."

As a survivor of childhood sexual abuse, I stand on the shoulders of all the other survivors and on the shoulders of those preceding who perished without having the opportunity to speak out. Daunting though it is, I am sensing from documented accounts and anecdotal stories that there is a feeling of empowerment in the air—that fresh air is beginning to blow in the direction of those stories yet untold. What a long way women and society on the whole have come, from the days of ridicule and scorn of one woman in testimony about sexual harassment by a prominent figure up for judicial confirmation, to a plethora of powerful figures routinely falling from grace because women from all strata of life have been finding their voice. What an era of empowerment! Is that your voice that I can hear resounding?

As you speak your stories and stand your ground, think of the millions across the globe whose lives will be radically changed because of your stories—indeed your courage!

Permit me to share a few survivor stories of other women who experienced childhood sexual abuse. Their names have been changed to protect their confidentiality. This is to give insight that this type of trauma is more prevalent than we know. Over the years having met and conversed with many women not included here, similar undesired behaviors that manifest in their social interactions were identified. As you read, if you are struggling with anything mentioned, you are not alone and can work through this, moving forward in powerful ways.

SURVIVOR 1
Why Me?

I am okay today; not sure where I will be mentally and emotionally during and after completing this questionnaire. I really don't feel like talking at this time. My abuse isn't something I like to discuss. Yes, I am still wrestling with lots of issues.

So, when did it begin? It started when I was around five years old, and my half-brother was the culprit.

I recall clearly several times that day he would molest me.

In my family's house in the Bronx there was a brown sofa pushed against a mirrored wall. The carpeting was red. I remember that. And I remember that day when I was lying face down on that brown sofa—no pants or undergarment on. It's coming back—his weight resting on me. His hands and his penis against my buttocks. My stomach is hurting from being pressed down. I stared at the red carpet, not understanding then or even now why or what was happening. But there was a milky substance he would wipe off the sofa after each time.

You asked me if I reported it. The answer is no. In fact, it wasn't until I was in my twenties that I could bring myself to say something. Whether or not my early childhood trauma affected my personal relationships as an adult, I am not quite sure. But I feel that my pattern of promiscuity in adult life might be linked to the childhood experience. But maybe this is something that could come out in counseling.

Let me say that the reason I have not sought counseling is because I am not ready to deal with that ugly part of my life. I have protected myself by blocking it out. I have shared my experience with close friends but never with professionals. I am so afraid of having to deal with the deep-down trauma if things begin to uncover.

Anger issues, lots of them! And I am inclined to hold things in. I know that in sharing my experience with my family—mom, dad and brother (not my half-brother)—nothing ever came of it. It was more or less "Sorry that happened" and left there. It was as if no one cared, and no consequences for it were given. So it has made me hold a lot of my feelings in about things that bother me, or things I have gone through or am going through. I have learned that my issues are mine and mine alone to deal with.

My half-brother recently passed away, and I felt numb about it. My fear of seeing him again or being alone with him is gone, but there is no closure. I will always question at times when the memory is triggered: "Why me?"

(An educated career woman with a beautiful family, this woman experienced trauma that has affected her life from youth into adulthood, as you have read. However, she has not cowered at life's challenges but is tenacious in not allowing the abusive experience to deter her from being a positive role model for her children and an influential person in all relationships. Become who God created you to be. —NM)

SURVIVOR 2
A Broken Crayon That Still Colors

My Lord, where do I begin?

My story of childhood sexual abuse started way back when I was about twelve, but you'd think someone would have cared enough and been astute enough to detect and save a young child from this debauchery.

It began as a child sexual assault case—inappropriate sexual touching, kissing my neck and such—and graduated to full-fledged molestation at the hands of my stepfather; then by his nephew, a political figure within the community, who I assumed would help when I told him; my teenage boyfriend; a male cousin; a female neighbor; a male best friend; my brother—even now, the list is playing on and on in my head.

Where did my childhood go? Is it a phase in my yet-to-be-lived life? At times I feel like a child is trapped on the inside waiting to jump out, to grab a jump rope and go outside to play. Other times I imagine myself as a little girl playing dollhouse with my favorite doll.

My stepfather—yes, my stepfather! The man who literally stepped on my prized possession: he stole my innocence! I guess that made me a vulnerable target, so much so that, when I was between sixteen and twenty-one years of age, my boyfriend jumped in on the deal!

Often, I feel stuck in a puddle of mud not really wanting to come out because I feel that's where I belong. Mud! Do you know what a puddle of mud looks like? It stains. It sticks on your clothes. It smells sometimes. I still hear my mother's voice in my head telling me, "You're nothing, and you will never amount to anything—a pretty face with an empty head!" (Here, the recorder pauses to exhale a bit as this sexually abused victim races through her flashbacks.)

There were no demeaning words that were off the table—you name it, it was hurled at me!

If it were possible to unpack the impact on my adult life, this is how I would explain it:

1. Fear.

2. Anxiety.

3. Attempted suicide.

4. Overprotective of my children (helicopter mom).

5. Inability to trust.

6. Inability to accept sincere love and affection.

7. Always choosing abusive men.

8. Promiscuity. Bisexuality. Difficulty with commitment in a monogamous relationship.

9. Becoming tired of people quickly and no longer wanting to be in a relationship with a man. Apprehensive of sustained relationships.

10. Needing to grieve the loss of the little girl that never grew up.

I'm not giving up on me, especially for my children. I live to see them happy. I believe there is light at the end of the tunnel. This is not where I stay stuck, because I still believe in God and trust him. From this experience a determination brews in me to be an example to others: I've been through it, and look where I am now. Goals were accomplished even when the battle in my mind provoked me to give up because professional success would not change the past. That ugly past developed my persistence.

SURVIVOR 3
Karen's Story

She tried everything she could think of to mummify her perpetrator. After her cute little hamster nipped her on her pinkie and caused some bleeding, she immediately changed its name to Monster. "Only monsters hurt little girls," she muttered to herself. She was floating back in time to when she was around ten and still in elementary school. "My teacher gave me a warning because I said boys were nasty." Karen recalled her teacher saying, "Some boys are actually very sweet." But Karen hated boys because they reminded her of grown men—like the man, her own father, who had molested her. She recalls that vividly, when she was only around eight and her father would take her for rides on his motorcycles. It started with her sitting behind him and clinching him tightly. "That was cool," Karen admits. But after a while her father insisted that, for safety purposes, she should sit in front of him. At about ten, now, Karen could tell something was not right. Her father would pull her in, tighter and tighter, and each time he did, the ride would get slower and slower, and then it became disgusting. That's as far as Karen would go about the ride—"Disgusting!"

Karen recalls that she and her mother got into a car accident on their way to school. The car was a mess, and Karen had to wear a neck brace or something like that for a couple weeks. Being home from school meant being alone with her father, who worked from home. Karen's dad endeared himself to his little girl even more. He was massaging her torso with his large hands and running his fingers down her spine and all the way in front and "eventually everywhere else," she recalls. "The feeling was odd and distasteful, but in some ways I struggled not to see his attention as [the actions of] a loving, caring father."

Karen continues: "Day after day, I would pray that my mother would figure out my odd feelings and help me. But she didn't, and I was terrified to say something."

Karen's dad had convinced her that each of them was helping the other—he giving her affection to make her feel good, and she in turn giving him pleasure to make him feel good. And things escalated from there until she was about fourteen and her father passed away from a massive heart attack. Only after he had passed away was she "free" to open up to her mother.

Now operating a successful legal practice, Karen is a star advocate for giving women of sexual abuse a voice. She feels freed and no longer lives being conquered by the past. In fact, she much prefers the term *survivor* rather than *victim.*—NM

***

May this brief selection of survivor stories encourage others to say something when they see or feel something.

Having experienced a similar fate, as friends, we reach out, listen to, discuss and strengthen each other. I hope that from these shared narratives you derive hope and healing to love yourself, forgive, and be courageous.

CHAPTER 4

The Value of a Good Friend

The wisdom of Naomi and the courage of Ruth!

For some people, friends come a dime a dozen, as the saying goes. However, for me, it is more like discovering just one single sincere friend was heaven-sent. That's what Heaven sent me!

I have a dear friend I have known since we were both eight years old. We raised our children together as bonded families. We cried together. We laughed together. My motto is: when one is down, the other must be able to raise up the other.

Like Ruth and Naomi from the Bible, we are inseparable—one is blessed with wisdom, and the other with abundant faith.

If you've never read the story of Ruth and Naomi and how they forged a beautiful, lasting friendship, I urge you to read it. I invite you to feast on the pages in the book of Ruth chapter 1. See how their story speaks to your heart.

Tragedy. Famine. The deaths of their spouses. Through it all, they stuck together, each sharing the challenges of the other. Neither had second thoughts of severing ties with the other.

How comforting it must have been to know that, though you are going through your crucible, you are knitted so tightly alongside a spiritually devoted friend.

I'm reviewing the poetic beats (stanzas) sent by Ruth to her precious mother-in-law, Naomi, words so important, and poignant, and heartfelt that they ended up in scripture in the book of Ruth.

Listen closely as Ruth assures her special God-sent friend and spiritual sister about their special friendship. "But Ruth replied: Don't urge me to leave you or to turn back from you. Where you go I will go, and where you stay I will stay. Your people will be my people and your God my God." (Ruth 1:16)

I have a spirit that connects easily with people. That's one of my blessings. "A cheerful heart is good medicine, but a crushed spirit dries up the bones." (Proverbs 17:22)

This has helped me to smile in those days when I am buffeted to and fro, seemingly with every puff of wind that blows. And I too have been blessed with soul sisters. There is one who is particularly near and dear to me. She listens. She prays. She consoles. And even during my feeble attempts to reconcile with my biological sister, this friend risked being pulled into a pond muddied with sensitive issues just to help keep my world from caving in.

You've been there! Those for whom you've done so much abandoning you in your hour of need! But I am indebted to God, as he provided that very "ram in the thicket." And if the reference piques your interest, you can read again the story of Abraham to understand how God shows up in the nick of time. And he will show up for you just when you are fiddling around the edges of life's circumstances.

Yes, I am alive to testify, unabashedly, that God provided astonishingly for me through friendships, and he will similarly provide for all those who trust him!

This is no gimmick!

Friendships! Choose them wisely, but choose them! You will need them!

Money can't buy them. Notoriety can't will them. They are once-in-a-lifetime precious gems cultivated over time, so handle them with care.

CHAPTER 5

Looking Back

L ooking back at a time when I was still in bows and bobby socks, I was forced to deal with keeping dark secrets. For a brief while, I believed in what was perpetrated upon me—the twisted mind of a naive child! If I had let out even a little bit to my young friend and it had become known, perhaps things would have been different.

But I am coming upon a beautiful place now where so much is retiring into memory of the past. I am glad to be here now, and I can't rewrite history or judge my journey as if I were an adult . . . I was a child making the best choices I could.

Compartmentalizing is a damaged child's best friend. It was mine! But to be vulnerable is even harder, though sometimes a blessed thing. For the more I crack open the window into my little dark room of secrets, the brighter the outer world seems to become. Friendships are becoming easier to foster, and I am finally beginning to find that rest amid the notes in my musical piece.

Though my interactions with people are still guarded, inch by inch I feel I'm getting there!

You meet me, and right away you can tell I'm a type A personality! Imagine a social butterfly having to conceal so much brightness and light and replace them with a subdued, guarded effect!

I still watch intently as kids are hugged by adults, particularly those of the opposite sex. I should be enjoying those kinds of gestures, but sometimes the memories, the chip on my shoulder, just get in the way. But this is why I struggle! This is my test! This is my reality! One day everything is moving along beautifully, until it is not! Occasional bouts of my troubled world show up—stark reminders of my painful past. My mood changes on the drop of a dime, and there we go again—vivid images of my violators making me suffer in the worst way.

As an adult, I can still hear, "Don't tell anyone." And I'm left with the thoughts of being a catalyst to the crime, recurrent in my mind. As I've become a bit more comfortable sharing these invading musings, I was told that I needed to "control my thoughts."

But that angered me all the more.

I just couldn't get over it. Something about adults pretending to know my pain just didn't sit right.

Under my breath I can hear myself even now: "Hypocrites!"

But it's a new day now as I scroll back to my cherished belief that God has a special purpose for every life he has caused to be born. And even though as a child I did not fully grasp this notion, there was a little something that constantly stood by as a silent witness: "Better is coming!"

So, as I develop and mature intellectually and spiritually, more and more I am determined to rise above the filth and horror that consumed so much of my earlier life. And the more I reflect on God's purpose for my life, the more empowered I become. So whenever those flashbacks of morbidity arise, I hold fast! I have a go-to goal and a go-to assurance: "My grace is sufficient for you, for my strength is made perfect in weakness. Therefore, I will boast all the more gladly about my weaknesses, so that Christ's power may rest on me. That is why for Christ's sake, I delight in weakness, in insults, in hardships, in persecutions, in difficulties. For when I am weak, then I am strong." (2 Corinthians 12:9–10) Jesus unleashes his perfect power, equipping me to do what I couldn't before: speak.

I Chose Selfishness

I am laughing now. Visible is the wrinkling of your forehead as you ask yourself, despite talks of a good God: Is she promoting selfishness? Yes! I chose me. I chose God's recommendation to be transformed by the renewing of my mind. (Romans 12:2) Sound intellect for reasoning and judgement is what our Heavenly Father has granted us. No one is defined by his or her perils unless internalized and lived. Past fears of transparency and vulnerability have been abandoned, arching the way for novelty exercising forgiveness. Today I convey and radiate confidence, content in the skin I'm in. The brain is an amazing organ; its functions can work for or against us. Research shows that what someone chooses to expend mental attention and energy on deepens the impression of its neural pathways. Choosing to shift the negative thoughts and accompanying undesirable emotions to positive ones, as by reciting biblical promises or prayers of thankfulness, aids in rewiring the brain. We cannot erase the past but could eradicate a tragic future by making prudent choices. Stay the course. Giving us freedom of choice, God subjected himself to our decisions to accept or reject his way of righteousness. Luke

17:1–2 states that offenses will occur among humanity, "but woe to him by whom the offense occurs; and whoever causes one of these little ones who believe in me to stumble, it would be better for him if a millstone were hung around his neck, and he were thrown into the sea, than that he should offend one of these little ones." I have accepted that I belong to God, and it doesn't matter how old I become, I am still his gem. In many arenas of life, we will interact with those whom childhood or any sexual trauma has not spared its painful aftermaths with negative manifestations. I hope that you and the significant people in your life grasp a better understanding that your battle is something larger than you could resolve on your own. Give it all to Jesus, and he will turn your sorrows into joy. Despite our afflictions, I pray that you too would feel his presence and trust His purpose.

CHAPTER 6

I'm Breaking the Silence:

The Need to Exhale

No longer wanting to be enslaved by fear of the shame and guilt that haunted me for many years, I knew it was time to release the dragon standing guard over my life. I needed to transition to a new prison guard—babysitting the secret was not strengthening me—my power had been outsourced! I knew all about God providing a ram in the thicket for Abraham—in fact, that's my favorite Genesis story! But would I be blessed with a similar experience?

I remember like yesterday hobnobbing with my Bible instructor, who was also a licensed social worker. Believe me when I tell you that the connection was instant, and very soon the reluctant and stifled voice had seemingly found its space. No timing is better than God's timing, for at an appointed time, he parted my lips and loosed my tongue to help dislodge my apprehensions.

My own mother bore witness, for the first time, to my years of hidden secrets. The terror in her eyes! Watching her, perhaps for the first time in her life, being at a loss for words! I could understand why, because I saw her hurt in her quietness. It was therapeutic for her as well—that was surprising! For it was a chance for her to unload. To hear her tell an instance when she unexpectedly caught my half-brother about to attempt the offense on my older sister and punishing him, enraged me. I know now what the truism means: people can't give you what they don't have, yet I felt she could have done so much more to shield me.

But nothing is so freeing like full disclosure. And now the groundwork has been laid for mother–daughter reconciliation and restoration. I pray for God's strength and wisdom to go forth in peace telling those dearest to me of the trauma and its impact. I'm openly and honestly telling friends and others who have shared their story with me that I too have been molested, and we now speak in-depth and tearfully and find it to be a cleansing process. I'm talking with people who tell me about others they were aware or suspicious of; I'm no longer ostracizing myself from my story. I embrace even the hard parts of my story because all the pieces fit perfectly, shaping who I am today. I pray that I will be connected with those that I could help. How can you break the silence in your life? *There is hope.*

There is a saying that there is strength in numbers. And if this is true, then perhaps the tide is beginning to turn in the direction of deterrence of the brutal crime of sexual assault and justice for the victims. Just as it is reported that it took thousands of attempts before the light bulb was invented, likewise the fact that sexual abuse is a crime that transcends all strata and all color and culture in society; so will this light begin to shine on all the heretofore-dark corners, and back rooms, and in every crevice where sunlight has been forbidden. Star athletes, Hollywood actors, teachers, presidents—powerful people who escaped the sunlight will now have to face their judgment. And to all those who might still feel powerless, as you navigate the mess you might be wading in, you will now breathe freer knowing that you too have been empowered by those brave souls who are, each day, turning on that light to flush out those in hiding.

Empowerment

If only society could find a way to stop the shaming of sexually abused survivors, then perhaps the floodgates will open and throngs of survivors will file out. Right now, the stigma that a survivor has to endure is sometimes just as bad as, if not worse than, the act of sexual abuse itself. So it's as if the survivor is twice victimized. That's one thing I had to get off my chest.

People look at you differently when they discover your story. And they ask questions like: Are you okay? Of course, I'm not okay! I've had something precious taken away! And that would have been my response as a child or young adult, if not for liaison with God my **Savior.** *Another of the questions you will hear asked of victims of sexual abuse is this: Why did it take you so long to speak up? I understand the question quite well because there is so much ignorance and lack of understanding in general about the highly sensitive nature of sexual abuse.*

The questions that arise are not like ones that appear on a pop quiz, nor on a true-or-false test. And there is no one-size-fits-all answer, because every single occurrence of sexual abuse has its own unique set of circumstances, and even the victims, though so similar, are so vastly different—in personality, background, and emotional and physical stamina. But there is one common thread inherent in all cases—no sexually abused victim ever asked to be degraded, humiliated, or abused—not one! And why the secret for so long? Unless you have walked a mile in a survivor's shoes, you will never truly understand the psychological influence a sexual abuser has on the victim. For that reason alone, every single sexually abused victim deserved to be heard, loud and clear.

If we talk about empowerment narrowly and in terms of after the fact, or solely in the context of male-bashing, or women survivors taking up arms and unleashing war on the opposite gender or even on their perpetrator, that could be counterproductive. So, for best results, let's look at empowerment twofold: first, empowerment for survivors who have been scorched and emotionally burned from the harsh affliction of sexual abuse who are clamoring for a voice and healing so they may live a life of normalcy; and second, equal empowerment for the parents (mothers in particular) of victims who perhaps condoned sexually abusive relationships between their young daughters and their abusers, whether for profit or because these mothers too had a history of abusive relationships which clouded their judgment and even caused them to sympathize with their child's abusers. These parents, too, need to be a part of the equation in terms of the empowerment of their girls in the healing process.

So, let's dig deeper into this issue of empowerment. For it is of little comfort to look at some celebrity case and take our eyes off our own problem right in our backyard, where it is so much easier to identify cause and effect. Actually, you don't need elaborate case studies and intricate discourse. Here is a case in point right here in the form of this question: Did you know that many sexual abuse cases are hatched in the family's backyard? Many! I've connected with dozens in person and in phone conversations. Thus, this is my appeal to families who are reeling from the internal struggle of the past: you will never be able to break free and heal yourself and your family until you stop the internal bleeding! Because you have been stuck in your echo chamber for such a long time, where the only things that resonate with you are the things you have been rehearsing over and over in your own mind, you are ill-equipped on your own to open up to new information. That's where professional help can make a world of difference. If only you could admit that you have been manipulated, and if only you could understand that a person who is manipulated isn't even aware that he or she has been brainwashed, another way of saying it. But the good news is that there is freedom and healing in exhaling. Just give yourself a chance to open the door, just a little.

I want to give you a peek into the world of some of the women who needed to exhale as I gathered insights for my book, sometimes from backyard fences. The trauma of losing one's virginity to a family member devastates a young girl as she enters puberty and matures through her teenage years and beyond, onto adulthood.

Here is what one of my mentors shared with me, and has given me permission to share with all of you, about an experience at a domestic violence and sexual assault workshop she conducted in 1999:

My mentor was invited to speak for Divine Worship Service that weekend. She arrived in the city the night before, slept in the comfortable bed at the head elder's home, and had a scrumptious breakfast, experiencing no apparent anxiety or any such thing.

On arrival at the worship center, she was escorted to the preparation room for prayer. Then it was time for her to walk onto the platform with the other participants. She prayed some more, then heard the theme song sung to the beautiful accompaniment on the organ, and she began to relax. As a matter of fact, she could scarcely wait to present what God had commissioned her to deliver.

It was Women's Day, and the church was packed with women of all colors, shapes, ages, and cultures; the audience was sizable, full of beautiful women in their adorable outfits—what an amazing gift from God!

"No More Vanilla Christians" was the sermon she had worked hard on putting together in the early mornings prior to the event.

Little did she know that there in the center section of the pews some of those same beautifully clad ladies had come not just to hear her preach, but to attend the domestic violence workshop she would conduct a couple hours later. Lunch happened in the fellowship hall right across from the Temple; then came the workshop, which began with the theme "End It Now" and a video presentation about women and their lives after domestic violence and sexual abuse.

The hall was filled to capacity with women and, surprisingly, quite a few men. My mentor had not interacted with this particular group before, and she thought that good if only because their expectations of her, she guessed, neutral, and hers of them were also neutral. But they were hospitable and warm, which put her at ease.

Over the years and as part of her routine, she met with event sponsors in a room for prayer before speaking. So, again, she proceeded with confidence that the outcome of the workshop was out of her hands and in God's.

Back inside the main hall, the women's ministries coordinator took to the podium to introduce my mentor, telling why she had come to town and why the video End It Now: No More Violence was chosen.

Relaying her experience, my mentor looked at me with a smile and voiced: "In a moment you will understand how when God has his hand in the mix, nothing is happenstance, and nothing is coincidental, but everything is divinely purposeful." She continued sharing that there in that very audience sat two ladies, perhaps in their early forties, who had attended Divine Worship and had spilled over into the fellowship hall for lunch and workshop. She noticed one of them was eager to be at the event because she was focused, pen and pad ready to make notes. The visual of that lady so incredibly tuned in as the video rolled had remained vivid in her memory to that day.

Like me, you are probably asking the question by now: What happened to the lady who stood out? Oh, did she have a story! My mentor informed me that she told about her church pastor and a full-blown sexual relationship with him at an early age. And after all those years, she was still seething because the church board and top administrators did everything they could to shoo her story and her away in order to protect the clergyman. But this all-grown-up professional vowed never to let her ordeal go away, and she promised that she will confront her "demons" at every turn by speaking out. This woman, she assumed, was probably in her twenties at the time of her abuse, yet for many years after her ordeal, she suffered in silence because someone she trusted, her pastor, had exploited her.

What an oxymoron! How could an occasion be so sad and yet so empowering? In retrospect, she understood why the enemy was hell-bent on knocking her feet from under her. He wanted her to skip out on a "waiting" congregation, a cathartic and long-to-be-remembered workshop.

In a sense, it's like finding the journey that's right for you. In spite of all you have gone through, and though the support for you is overwhelming, people, though well-meaning, will come and go, but you have to champion your own cause. **You have to dig deep and scoop up the wherewithal to lift yourself up onto your own two feet; that's where your greatest empowerment lies.** *In a sense, it's like mourning the loss of a close loved one. The sentiments and condolences are in high gear. The flowers and cards fill the den. The hugs and kisses and words of sympathy are appreciative. But once the videotaping is over and the mourners leave the cemetery and return to their individual places of residence, what you are left with is your own shoulders to bear you up.*

Though well-meaning, you cannot expect others to be your hand and foot—they cannot always be there at your beck and call. So here is a partial solution: People grieve differently. People process things differently. And you? You have to find your own therapist.

You have to find the right associates, build your own support team. You have to find your own route to healing—I pray that you do! Find your way to Jesus and give him the key to your heart. "Draw near to God and he will draw near to you." (James 4:8)

CHAPTER 7

Overcoming and Becoming

Nothing is impossible with God!

So when we reflect on the roller-coaster whys and wherefores of life—and if, like me, you've moved from crisis to crisis—we need to understand that true healing is possible, but it can only come from God, the ultimate healer, and only through a full surrender.

I am a witness that God is able to take us from a place of surrendering to the wishes of the enemy who seeks to destroy, to full surrender to a God who is able. The truth is that because God loves us so much, he is not willing that anyone who trusts him be turned away with issues unresolved.

That, in a nutshell, is my view of forgiveness!

Forgiveness moves you out of victim mode.

Forgiveness settles the scores that lead to emotional and physical bondage.

Forgiveness draws you farther and farther away from your abuser and closer to the Father.

Forgiveness frees you to worship the Lord in the beauty of holiness.

Forgiveness is what God grants to his children every day, as often as they ask of him.

So, as I speak with a now unchained voice, I need to make one thing perfectly clear—I am bound to forgive my perpetrators, yet in no way am I releasing them from the terror and harm they inflicted on my young life.

My singular prayer is that they will move toward accountability and surrender so that they may be forgiven by their Creator. I needed to release anger and shame which had united in an unholy matrimony within my heart following my abuse. I discovered I had taken on an issue for which I no longer have vigor. Until I surrendered myself and the predicament over to God's reins, I was unable to completely forgive and move forward.

It is possible—I pray it will happen! For when we understand that the stench of our sins is no match for God's mercy, nothing is impossible; therefore, we must never allow our sins to become greater than God's grace.

Dear God, As I march along in the healing process, I want to also pray for the salvation of my perpetrators. This moment is a watershed moment, Father. So in humble pleadings and mindful of my own failures, I pray that you will look into the hearts of the ones who have wronged me so terribly. Snatch them, I pray, from the jaws of the enemy. Make their hearts susceptible to your voice. May they find in you a safe space to lean. And just as you have done for others in times past, I pray that you will give them the victory again and again. Father, lift the cloud of shame and guilt. May my own song of your amazing grace be theirs. Set them free in Jesus' name. Amen.

What do you need to release, to forgive, and to give over to God to free you?

CHAPTER 8

When Statistics Are Fake

The numbers are staggering! Child sexual abuse is prevalent, but lack of reporting impacts actual cases, since many children disclose their experience in adulthood (*Resources for Victims of Child Sexual Abuse and Their Families,* updated May 19, 2022) Furthermore, the World Health Organization reports that 150 million girls and 73 million boys worldwide have experienced child sexual abuse.

There is a sobering public service commercial out there that ends with this: "When life gives you a wake-up call, answer it!"

Here we are, World, asleep at the wheel of an infested culture of silence! Our little girls and boys are sitting ducks for depraved adults to shoot, and everyone else is sound asleep!

The sirens are going off.

Is anyone listening?

The alarms on the cell phones are sounding.

Would someone please press accept?

Emergency vehicles are screaming nonstop, speeding down the streets to rescue the next child from the clutches of some perpetrator!

Will motorists please clear the way?

We hear the screams of innocence in those blaring sounds—wake-up calls we so often miss, or perhaps we hear them, we identify them, but we turn a blind eye.

Or, does even God hear the cries of little children? Does he even care?

These are perfectly fair questions, for where was God when I was cornered by my perpetrators?

These were the questions of a little girl, but there is another question.

Recently I read a piece in *The Atlantic,* "America Has an Incest Problem," and all the way down in the middle of the piece I was confronted by the thousand-pound elephant in the room—"Why do incest victims stay silent for so long?"

As I read this question, I became tense.

Do people not understand the depth of shame that incest and sexual assault victims face?

I looked at the research.

I read the Penn State accounts.

I studied the sexual abuses in the Catholic Church.

I read about the betrayal of pastor–parishioner trust. "In November 2020, New York's Attorney General filed a lawsuit against the Buffalo Catholic Diocese, alleging its leaders protected priests accused of child sex abuse. The diocese has pledged 'full cooperation' with authorities" (BBC, "New York Attorney General sues Buffalo Diocese for 'sex abuse cover-up'," October 5, 2021). This is by no means the only religious institution inflicting harm on children.

But these accounts merely scratch the surface, and I'll be presumptuous enough to dare anyone—just begin sharing your story, and watch all the hurting women and sometimes men come out of the shadows! The line will snake around the block.

I chuckled!

I squirmed!

I scratched my head!

I became agitated!

The numbers don't begin to scratch the surface. So many stay silent and never share their story. These numbers are just from the shared cases. Who knows how many victims never come forward, their numbers never counted? I can tell you: too many.

We need answers. We need a safe house for victims to unload their burdens.

We need to unmask the terror of incestuous acts, and we need to make it respectable for victims to tell somebody without being victimized over and over again.

And what else do we need? We need parents who are more attentive to the welfare of their children—parents who are equipped to create trusting bonds between themselves and their children so that childhood secrets become a thing of the past.

I Hated to Go Home

Home?

I hated the word *home!*

Put that word on pause for a minute while I ask those who would sit in judgment over my question.

I forgot—home is where the heart is. But, in my case, home was where my woes began—in fact, my whole neighborhood was the elusive accomplice to my pain.

As I was making emotional preparation to tell what is only a part of my story, bits and pieces that had long since lodged in my stored-away memory, I asked myself over and over again why I felt for so long that no one really cared about sheltering me from the vicissitudes of life. Then all of a sudden, like refreshing a computer when it is stalled, I allowed verses of an old hymn—written by a Methodist pastor, Frank E. Graeff, as he was suffering bouts of depression—to resuscitate my spirit:

Does Jesus care when my heart is pained

Too deeply for mirth or song,

As the burdens press, and the cares distress

And the way grows weary and long?

Does Jesus care when my way is dark

with a nameless dread and fear?

As the daylight fades into deep night shades,

does He care enough to be near?

Oh yes, He cares, I know He cares,

His heart is touched with my grief;

When the days are weary, the long nights dreary,

I know my Savior cares.

Even as you are reading this with me, pretty little cute girls and sometimes boys are living in hell—there is little to no daylight between themselves and ending it all. Fortunately, the truth is there is one who cares for them—the same one who carried me on his shoulders from among those thick ugly bushes and even within our home in my island nation to help me become a diligent woman of the word.

Oh yes, he cares—I know he cares, and Jesus will raise up many Natashas to fight for you! "Carry each other's burdens, and in this way, you will fulfill the law of Christ." (Galatians 6:2) The courage that I now possess enables me to stand up for myself and others. What are you willing to stand and fight for?

CHAPTER 9

The Jerusalem Stretch: Nearing Home!

A t one point, I said enough is enough! I was ready to wipe clean the frosted glass window that had been obscuring my vision.

It was about time!

For too long, the "locusts" had been gnawing away at my most productive years; and I had read somewhere that God had a unique way of restoring those years.

That perked me up!

Now I could embrace that special promise in 1 Peter 2:9 written especially for me: "You are a royal priesthood, a chosen generation." Thus, in 2020—New Year's Eve to be exact—my prayer was that God would do whatever it took to make me fit for service.

Truth be told, I prayed that prayer with reservations and actually second-guessed whether I had been biting off more than I could chew. For what if God had answered and assigned me to a difficult task?

But the desire to obey was so much greater than my reservations.

During this same period, I recall listening to a sermon. It was a brisk fall Sunday. God and an unsuspecting Abraham in a meeting—that's big-time stuff!

And when I read it for myself in Genesis 12:1–2, I pictured Abraham doing his normal chores when he received a visit from God, who told him to relocate to a different place.

I have read this chapter in Genesis 12 over and over again, and each time Abraham's faith never ceases to amaze me.

You can't even make a case and say that there was a conversation or a dialog between God and Abraham.

It was more like a don't-talk-back-at-me instruction.

Just pack up and leave?

Abraham hadn't a clue where he was going.

How many of us could handle that?

Abraham could not have known, because God seemingly and on purpose, did not tell him.

Perhaps God hinted?

If you could call "a place" a hint!

Let's read the verse to get a fuller picture: The LORD had said to Abram, "Go from your country, your people and your father's household to the land I will show you. I will make you into a great nation, and I will bless you; and I will make your name great and you will be a blessing."

But here is the rub!

From all accounts, Abraham was a responsible family man, so you might think he would ask God to send his family to join him later on.

Abraham did none of that. In fact, scripture doesn't even record that he asked God to protect his family in his absence.

Abraham, like an obedient child to a father, began the journey.

Conditions didn't matter.

Length of stay didn't matter.

Survival of his business didn't matter.

The next morsel of food didn't matter.

Abraham obeyed!

So, as we are nearing home, I told myself there are dos and don'ts along the way. God has a platform reserved for my story, but first I have to be receptive to his leading.

Here we go with today's Venn diagram! We have Abraham's model of obedience in one place, and at the other end of the spectrum we have Jonah, a powerful preacher–prophet who, because he hated his assignment, decided to get into a debate with God about it—two sets of instructions, with two completely different outcomes!

One of my go-to scripture verses on obedience comes in handy! It is perfect for my promise to God to send me "wherever" he wishes.

"See, I set before you today life and prosperity, death and destruction. For I command you today to love the LORD your God, to walk in obedience to him, and to keep his commands, decrees and laws; then you will live and increase, and the LORD your God will bless you in the land you are entering to possess." (Deuteronomy 30:15–16)

I am battling with my mind now. For I have no desire to limp towards God when he commissions me—I want, like Abraham, to have unquestionable faith.

You probably guessed what's coming next!

To compound my anxiety after my request of God, the enemy upped the ante.

I'm in the home stretch now, and conflicts both at home and in the workplace heated up. But here is some good news! Though the enemy raised the stakes, God's grace favored me. I stuck with my desire to be faithful to God! The enemy shook my faith but couldn't upend my story.

I prayed on.

I sang hallelujah songs.

I read my Bible.

I trusted God!

In moments of doubts and second-guessing, what do you do?

CHAPTER 10

Your War Chest or Your Tool Chest

In moments of doubts and second-guessing, I believe that is the time for you to go to your war chest or tool chest. This is where you keep your pick-me-up stories of truth and encouragement—words that inspire you and are soothing to your heart and spirit. It is where you keep practices and tools that uplift you and help you hold fast to the truth and keep stepping forward powerfully.

You can add to your war chest pick-me-upper stories like that of Paul, a servant of God who you will encounter elsewhere in this memoir, with his watershed conversion on the Damascus Road, and after he had devoted the remainder of his life to the saving of souls.

Paul could never have known that he would hold such a prominent role in God's army. What a thought! But he learned the mind-blowing lesson that God will equip those whom he calls.

It is true that Paul struggled like I do, like we all do even after God has done a makeover on us. Yet he trusted God. For though after his conversion Paul was a changed man, he had his moments. For here we find him lamenting over his struggles, "a thorn in his flesh". "For the good that I would I do not, but the evil which I would not, that I do." (Romans 7:19).

Clearly, God did not erase Paul's biological makeup—he transformed it! And the warring inside Paul tells me something else. It tells me that your journey and mine to eternity is a continuous one—that as long as we live, we submit and grow, and the more we submit to God's plan, the more we become like Christ. And the more we become like Christ, the more grace he extends for the journey.

So what did God do with Paul's strong-willed, scrappy personality? He used this bloodthirsty killer-man drive. He used it to drive sinners from the pit of Hell to a place called Heaven.

What a God who can transform a wretch like Paul to a powerhouse in ministry! Then that same God can raise up a humble girl, whose life had been torn apart at an early age, and fit her up for service!

I smile at this because you and I have a chance at God's amazing grace—if only we would embrace it when God confronts us on our Damascus Road! We too can use our voices in the marketplace being assured that God will make up all our biological inadequacies if we submit to him.

What stories inspire you? What practices help you stay grounded in truth and empower you to weather storms in your life? Strategies I use for spiritual grounding are deep breathing, visual imagery, counseling, journaling a source of release, heart-to-heart talks with trusted close friends and relatives, and including exercise as part of my routine. I awaken at five each morning to pray, worship in songs and study God's word with sound assurance of his guiding presence. Ultimately I believe the promises rooted in his word. He is the vine, and I am his branch, abiding in and sustained by him to bear fruit.

Fruit-Bearing: Two Trees, Different Outcomes

I told this story before about two fruit trees, a peach and an apple tree in our backyard in New York. You have probably seen fruit trees . . . and these two fruit trees taught me a powerful lesson.

I paid attention to them nearly every day, and especially during bearing season. It might have been the great soil they were growing in, but the trees were beautiful—like a home and garden magazine.

You don't have to be that old to know the thrill of picking a juicy peach or apple straight from the tree into your mouth.

I was in the backyard with a basket in hand. I didn't need a ladder or any props—the fruits were hanging nice and low. So I began picking to my heart's content.

It's hard to think negatively about beautiful fruits like the ones I harvested. Huge. Smooth. Color-perfect. It was a big deal!

The peaches were downright delicious. I was anticipating hearing my teeth crunch into one of the beautiful apples. But first I needed to peel it. It's just a bad habit of mine. I am aware that the most nutrients are sealed inside the skin, but bad habits die hard, they say.

And here is where the story takes a different route—I must have cut into a dozen apples, and every single one had been infested with parasites and cankerworms or some other destructive pests. They looked beautiful on the outside but were infested and rotting on the inside. Have you ever noticed this in your own life or in the lives of others?

Things can look beautiful and glorious on the outside . . . but very different when you pull back the outer layer and look at what lies beneath.

Jesus had an interesting observation about fruits. Perhaps he was talking about my apple and peach trees. I know for a fact he was talking about people, possibly Christians, when he lectured about fruit-bearing.

In Matthew 7:19, Jesus voiced this moving caution about the fate of a tree that bears bad fruit: it is cut down and discarded as useless. "Every tree that does not bear good fruit is cut down and thrown into the fire."

My apple tree could fit Christ's template for non-productive people who may look the part but on the inside are void of substance—their fruit is false.

They have learned a few things about God from Bible recitation.

They are the first in the temple and the last to leave.

They dress the part in modest outfits.

They may even have welcoming smiles.

But sadly, their hearts are far from God!

Remember the point—we have to clean up our dysfunctions, whatever they are, so that God can fit us for service.

A nice-looking coat of paint can't do it.

A fresh haircut won't work; neither will the most expensive cologne or perfume.

When God examines us, here is what he wants to see: a heart that has been cleansed by his precious blood—period!

A mind that is renewed. A fruit that is beautiful inside and out. This is the deal the Savior makes with all of us. He will accept no less!

I am searching my heart now to see if it's beating on God's stethoscope. Imagine that! But as I do, he quickly leads me to the parable of the fig tree, for yes, he is the Master Gardener.

I want to see what he has to say about a barren fig tree that stood for a long time with no fruit. Year after year, and season after season, still it bore no fruit.

Note the first line that pops out at me in Luke chapter 13: "No branch can bear fruit by itself unless it remains on the vine." So what does the Master do? He shows up armed with specific garden tools. We could only imagine what they are, but we are assured that they are fit for the pruning.

So he tenderly prunes, and clips, and trims off the dead portions of our lives. He even turns on the sprinkler system to water those dried-out patches.

What is he doing here? Why is he using garden tools? Why is he so meticulous?

Don't miss the point!

The vine he created was for the purpose of staying rooted and bearing fruit through him. He reminds us: "This is to my Father's glory, that you bear much fruit, showing yourselves to be my disciples." (John 15:8)

Imagine the joy in God's eyes as he watches his master-piece growing new shoots, ready to spread the joyful news that Jesus saves, and saves to the utmost all who, despite their past, present themselves for pruning and excavation.

CHAPTER 11

Surrendering Worldly Cares

"What's taking front and center of my affection?" I ask myself.

Stocks and bonds?

Get-rich-quick schemes?

A big house in an affluent neighborhood?

Expensive cars?

Nonstop rigorous climbing to the top of the corporate ladder?

Are these things choking me like they are choking the world?

Are they competing with God for prominence in my life?

Where am I on this list of priority options?

Why Am I Here?

I recently stumbled across a book title somewhere: *Why Am I Here?* The title intrigued me! So I paused long enough to turn the spotlight into my own soul. Long enough to ask that same question of myself: Why am I here? Is it just to fit in, or does God really have a special and unique plan for my life?

Television commercials fascinate me! Is it perhaps because they often have buried within them meaning far beyond their original intent?

Here's the question one Capital One Card commercial asks: "What's in your wallet?"

And the American Express Card, almost as if would not be left out, in another commercial advises: "Don't leave home without it!

I am in my study now, and the Capital One Card and the American Express Card commercials are still playing in my head. How do they fit into some other compelling spiritual truths? For these are the ones I depend on both for encouragement and for sustainability. Truths like Revelation 14:12: "Here is the patience of the saints; here are they who keep the commandments of God and the faith of Jesus."

And I could walk boldly and confidently because of John 3:16: "For God so loved the world that he gave his only begotten son, that whosoever believes in him should not perish but have everlasting life."

For the first time, I am understanding that Jesus really wants all to ignore the wrinkled clothes, the scuffs on the shoes, the tangles in the hair. I am understanding what's really important—that no one comes to Jesus all fixed up, yet no one leaves unchanged!

So, as I strive to divorce myself from worldly cares and focus on my future home, where sorrows and heartaches and pain and questionings will be nonexistent, I yield to David, the "man after God's own heart," who speaks so powerfully in Psalm 25:4–5, not from a place of mere platitudes but from a heart that was broken, chiseled, and reconstructed by the grace and mercy of God: "Show me your ways O Lord; teach me your paths, lead me in your truth and teach me, for you are the God of my salvation; on you I will wait all the day." May the depth of our love for God grow fortified roots harnessed against his naked truth.

Oh For a Faith to Serve the Lord!

What has the journey been teaching me?

"God has given to each man a measure of faith." (Romans 12:3) I needed to hold on to this! I needed to believe that even if God decided not to erase all the horrible memories of my past, I still need to exercise patience, believing that the God I trust is actively positioning me. For as he promises: "For I know the plans I have for you,' declares the Lord, 'plans to prosper you and not to harm you, plans to give you hope and a future." (Jeremiah 29:11)

Of course, there are periods of emotional disturbances in my soul! Of course, I ask the question every now and then: God, where are you?

So, what do I do? I continue to trust the One who has stuck with me and rescued me from the evil hands of my perpetrators and has allowed me to tell my story of deliverance!

And about my daily struggle to overcome?

I hang in there!

Paul's story of how he wrestled with a "thorn" in his flesh (2 Corinthians 12:7–9) teaches me to hang in there. It also teaches me that the "whys" are perfectly fine. For as powerful a man of God as he was, Paul had his moments of frustration with the "slow" process of deliverance.

I read Paul's frustrated uttering, and what grips me more than anything else is his emphasis on the number of times he asked God to strip away the "thorn" in his flesh. And each time God's response was the same. "My grace is sufficient."

A template for my own questionings? Could it be?

Perhaps, and yes! For here is what I know: Already God is beginning to equip me for greater ministry.

Already I can see the shards from the chiseling process begin to fall off. Not all of them at once, but bit by bit.

And for the rest?

God's grace is finishing those off too. It is this grace that will keep me strong along the road to becoming all that God wants me to be.

CHAPTER 12

My Prayer For You

My prayer for you, is that you keep taking steps— "that he who began a great work in you will complete it until the day of Jesus." (Philippians 1:6) "So, if the Son sets you free, you are free, indeed." (John 8:36)

I continue to remember the precious promises. For as I look back at my dysfunctional past, and the thorns and thistles I've had to negotiate along the way—the anger and unresolved vitriol I have subconsciously smuggled into my heart space—I am experiencing a "praise the Lord" moment that they have now taken a back seat to the beautiful testimonies that have emerged from my trials. And they will for yours too as you keep taking steps.

And like an old borrowed story about the lowly caterpillar that one day was transformed into a beautiful butterfly, that is my prayer for you and me.

I know my story is halfway complete. The fact is that out of a dismal background and a seemingly untenable plight, God spotted me in the distance, called me out by name, and positioned me to do great exploits for him.

The journey is very much a work in progress, but isn't that what it is all about? A consistent pressing on, until one day the journey will be complete and God will render me "faithful."

What a welcome respite that will be!

If you are having more questions than answers, know this—God can put you back together again! How he does it is so much like a contract between you and God. God presenting the facts of the agreement, and you sign the instrument in the affirmative.

What a breathe-in-breathe-out moment!

And even though history can never be altered, God will use history to do something even more beautiful: he will scoop up the pieces of a shattered, broken dream and make it become a legacy for mankind and for the glory of God.

So, God, because I believe you are there, reveal yourself faithful to your promises to every reader, that despite all the evil around us in this world, you are still God—you are the same God who searched the Samaritan woman's heart and sent her away with a message of hope; or the God who dumbfounded the accusers who wanted the adulteress woman stoned. You did not let public pressure dissuade you, but in your mercy you saved this dear woman from condemnation.

And look what you did for your daughter, Natasha! You chased after me like a doting father chases after his toddler child who is heading full-steam-ahead for the swimming pool. You grabbed her! You hoisted her upon your shoulder just like you did the lost sheep. And you brought her safely home.

What a good Shepherd you are! How generous you are with your love and compassion!

And now I pray for those precious lives that have been damaged by rape, incest, and other violent acts of sexual abuse, And for the millions who will read these pages. I want to look you in the eye—you need to know something—God can heal you! But as scripture reminds us: "Not by might nor by power, but by my Spirit,' says the Lord Almighty." (Zechariah 4:6 NIV)

"May the God of hope fill you with all joy and peace as you trust in him, so that you may overflow with hope by the power of the Holy Spirit." (Romans 15:13) Become empowered by participating in activities that aren't typical.

CHAPTER 13

Lessons I Learned From My Counseling Sessions

1. You must decide to heal. Much like an alcoholic who wants to quit drinking, the sexually abused victim must be open to help. Readiness to be rid of the bondage is acknowledging you were violated and desire release for a healthier way of living, employing skillful strategies.

2. Don't impede healing by processing everything alone. Long-lasting effects of trauma manifest itself in unhealthy habits in attempts to preserve one's functional mental state. So I encourage you to build a team of people to support you on your journey.

3. Disclose. Air your hurt. Pent-up feelings only retard the healing process. The pushback you get is more than worth the race to the finish line. But don't rush to disclose all at once—you may have to do it in increments.

4. Don't get stuck in denial. You have been wronged, period! Own your hurt and accept help. Believe your feelings are valid, and address them with support that promotes your growth.

5. Understand it wasn't your fault. Victims, particularly children, tend to blame themselves for their

predicament. Place the blame where it belongs—on the abuser.

6. It's okay to be angry! Don't let anger make you overly negative. Use it to help you process your pain.

7. Forgive yourself. Forgiveness releases you from self-blaming and shaming. And as you heal, move toward forgiving your abuser. This may not happen all at once, but as it does, you will find that it is something good for you.

8. Find value in your spirituality. People who are attached to a faith-based church can benefit from solid pastoral care.

9. Get professional help. Find a credible professional Christian counselor.

10. While you don't need an army of people around you, socializing with friends is good therapy; but be careful not to use alcohol or drugs to kill your pain.

11. Pray. Never underestimate the value of prayer. Miracles happen when we pray.

12. Take care of yourself. Rest. Exercise. Pamper yourself with a spa visit now and then. Self-care promotes relaxation, improves confidence, builds self-esteem, and reduces pain and stress. When you care for yourself it enables you to care for and about others with a clear mind and physical capacity. Being overwhelmed does not equate to a healthy lifestyle. "Come to Me, all you who labor and are heavy laden, and I will give you rest. Take My yoke upon you and learn from Me, for I am gentle and lowly in heart, and you will find rest for you souls." (Matthew 11:28–29) Obtaining

balance in taking time for yourself, is not selfish. Jesus recharged and prepared for his tasks by spending time away from his disciples and the multitudes who came to listen and obtain healing: "So He himself often withdrew into the wilderness and prayed." (Luke 5:16)

13. Since Jesus, our role model, exemplified His need for the Father, so too is our need for spiritual sustenance; staying close to the Father enables us to live more deeply and fully. Become one with your creator in mind, body and soul. "Because God is true and faithful, His thoughts for you are precious and are more numerous than the sands of . . ." (Psalms 139:17–18) In the back of the book I've included some powerful scriptures to support you on your journey; they encourage my heart, and I hope they do the same for yours.

You are stronger than you think. As you make progress, you will experience more awareness, integration, and compassion. You will gain the ability to move toward a better future.

An appeal to parents and guardians

- LOVE your children, and love them well. See to it that the bond with your child is airtight. Leave no room for intruders. A victim's desire for love and affection is the primary thing that captures the perpetrator's attention.

- Keep an awareness of your child's expressions of emotion. It will provide insight into distress affecting your child's vulnerable mind.

- Resist the temptation to be overly confident. It is true that your child may be as smart as a whiz, but a child is still a child! Have you ever wondered why perpetrators often use lollipops to lure their young victims? It is because kids will be kids—kids like sweet things, and kids like gifts. They lack the ability to see what's lurking behind the first taste or the pretty wrapper on the package.

- Educate yourself. When a child is sexually abused, that abusive act is just the beginning of years of a challenging life. So many of them gravitate to a life of prostitution. Many gravitate to drugs and alcohol. Many of them revert to a world of sexual abuse once again. Many of them have serious issues developing and sustaining intimacy in their relationships. Sadly, many sexually abused children give up on people, and society, and life, and commit suicide.

So how else are we to behave as parents and guardians?

We erect another wall, a first wall—a wall around our children's hearts, and souls, and minds. We yield not to our own understanding, but we look to the one who blesses us with vision and discretion to shield our children from the predators of this world.

We owe it to our children, and we owe it to God. For guess what? What do you think is the one burning question in the heart of God about your children, ultimately and finally, and down the road? It is my scripture prayer for you. Receive it!

"Father, I want those you have given me to be with me where I am, and to see your glory, the glory you have given me because you loved me before the creation of the world." (John 17:24)

***

To all the readers of this book, this is a pivotal moment for you: You can rise above it! Don't blame yourself, but take responsibility for your own future, and move on, knowing that no good deed goes unrewarded, and no bad deed goes unpunished. You are in the Master's hand, and you are in the Master's plan! ~With love, Natasha

CLOSING REMARKS

God loves us with an everlasting love, so I'm deliberate in my actions to serve him. Many people question: if there is a loving God, why didn't he intervene to prevent the abuse? It was in the feelings of lowliness and questioning that God pressed in. Acknowledging his presence, I am learning to reflect on parenting mistakes and to give myself grace from messing up, speaking in a harsh tone towards my husband, feeling frustrated and overwhelmed, and losing my temper over trivial matters. God is glorified when self is removed and his power is unleashed. Trials can be disheartening, leaving us anxious and depressed, but Philippians 4:6 says, "Be anxious for nothing, but in everything, by prayer and supplication with thanksgiving let your requests be made known to God, and the peace of God that surpasses all understanding, will guard your hearts and minds through Christ Jesus." He shows up right on time and refreshes your mind with a different outlook: that God didn't turn his back. Where the spirit of the Lord is, there is freedom.

Thank you for reading my story, and I hope and pray it has encouraged you. For those of you who have yet to heal, know that it is this freedom and joy that I wish for you. Know that you are loved and valued. I am holding space for you each step of your journey. May your steps be filled with grace and covered in mercy.

APPENDIX 1

Your Go-To Scriptures

Because the Sovereign LORD helps me, I will not be disgraced. Therefore have I set my face like flint, and I know I will not be put to shame. (Isaiah 50:7 NIV)

May the God of hope fill you with all joy and peace as you trust in him, so that you may overflow with hope by the power of the Holy Spirit. (Romans 15:13 NIV)

Instead of your shame you will receive a double portion, and instead of disgrace you will rejoice in your inheritance. And so you will inherit a double portion in your land, and everlasting joy will be yours. (Isaiah 61:7 NIV)

Those who look to him are radiant; their faces are never covered with shame. (Psalm 34:5 NIV)

"...For I know the plans I have for you," declares the LORD, "plans to prosper you and not to harm you, plans to give you hope and a future." (Jeremiah 29:11 NIV)

Therefore, if anyone is in Christ, the new creation has come: The old has gone, the new is here! (2 Corinthians 5:17 NIV)

[B]eing confident of this, that he who began a good work in you will carry it on to completion until the day of Christ Jesus. (Philippians 1:6 NIV)

You intended to harm me, but God intended it for good to accomplish what is now being done, the saving of many lives. (Genesis 50:20 NIV)

See to it that no one falls short of the grace of God and that no bitter root grows up to cause trouble and defile many. (Hebrews 12:15 NIV)

But you, God, will bring down the wicked into the pit of decay; the bloodthirsty and deceitful will not live out half their days. But as for me, I trust in you. (Psalm 55:23 NIV)

Resources to Help

Don't suffer in silence. Get support, find valuable resources, and find the tools to help you heal. And when you're ready, share your story so other adult survivors of child sexual abuse know they're not alone.

In the US:

RAINN.org's National Sexual Assault Hotline:
1-800-656-HOPE (4673)

The Childhelp National Child Abuse Hotline:
https://childhelphotline.org (live chat)
1-800-422-4453 (call or text)
Or call your local police.

In Canada:

List of crisis lines for those affected by gender-based violence:
https://women-gender-equality.canada.ca/en/gender-based-violence/crisis-lines.html

List of family violence resources, services, and crisis lines:
https://www.canada.ca/en/public-health/services/health-promotion/stop-family-violence/services.html

In Australia:

1800RESPECT, the national domestic, family and sexual violence support service:
https://www.1800respect.org.au (online chat)
1800 737-732 (phone)

In England and Wales:

Rape Crisis:
https://rapecrisis.org.uk/get-help/ (online chat)
0808-802-9999 (24/7 rape and sexual abuse support line)

Victim Support:
https://www.victimsupport.org.uk/help-and-support/get-help/ (live chat)
08 08 16 89 111 (24/7 support line)

In Scotland, Ireland, and beyond:

Rape Crisis:
https://rapecrisis.org.uk/get-help/
support-outside-of-england-wales/

Victim Support Scotland:
https://victimsupport.scot
0800 160 1985

Victim Support Ireland:
https://www.victimsupportni.com

About the Author

Natasha McCoy is a licensed occupational therapist, providing compassionate service professionally in this capacity.

She earned both her master of science in occupational therapy and her bachelor of science in applied psychology at New York University, preceded by her associate's in arts with honors at Borough of Manhattan Community College. Natasha has worked in settings such as hospitals, acute care and inpatient rehabilitation, mental health, skilled nursing facilities, pediatric outpatient clinic, school and home care, performing home evaluations, community re-entry and wheelchair assessments; professional development of level one and level two students. Before beginning her career in occupational therapy, Natasha was a special education Head Start preschool teacher in New York City.

Natasha returned to and resided in Trinidad for four years, from 2013 to 2017, joining a small team of clinicians who provided therapy that was under-resourced on the twin islands. She was also an advocate for autism awareness, the Cerebral Palsy Association, and government support for people with disabilities.

She also operated a private practice, The Occupational Therapy Sanctuary, located in St. Joseph, Trinidad, where she evaluated and treated adults and pediatric clients presenting with various congenital and acquired cognitive and physical disabilities; simultaneously, she started and directed the preschool Learners' Sanctuary. She became a trained lecturer and student advisor for the first master's in occupational therapy program on the island, being licensed both in Trinidad and Tobago and the United States. While residing in Trinidad as a healthcare professional, Natasha functioned as a:

Member: Council of Professions Related to Medicine in Trinidad and Tobago.
Member: Board of Speech Language Therapy and Occupational Therapy in Trinidad and Tobago
Member: Association of Caribbean Occupational Therapist (ACOT)
Member: Trinidad and Tobago Occupational Therapy Association (TTOTA)

Achievements:
Editor's Choice Award from The National Library of Poetry, 1997
Faculty Honors Award for Academic Performance (Dean's List), 1999

Faculty Honors Convocation Award for Academic Performance, 2003

She currently resides in Florida. She is a Christian author, a wife, and the mother of five children.

Facebook: Natasha Roxy McCoy
LinkedIn: Natasha McCoy
Instagram: Natmccoynovels
Email: Natashamccoynovels@gmail.com

Reviews

"This riveting book will have you turning pages quickly as Natasha takes you through her experiences and that of other abuse survivors. Steps of Grace, Ladder of Mercy tells the story of women fighting to heal the little girl inside them who was abandoned and mistreated in their time of greatest need. This is a must-read for anyone who's been through sexual abuse, who feels lost, broken, and like they are the only ones going through the ups and downs of recovery. There is hope for restoration and complete healing as this amazing book shares time and again."

—Dr. Elizabeth Clamon
https://ElizabethClamon.com

"Natasha's book *"Steps of Grace, Ladder of Mercy"* is a beautifully written story about how child sexual abuse can destroy a person's thinking about who they are and their ability to function as a normal person in society. She describes perfectly how trauma affects each person and how these lasting effects change the course of a person's life. She uses scriptures to help strengthen her faith in herself and her purpose going forward. As a fellow child sexual abuse survivor, reading her words about encouragement and perseverance lifted me up and helped me know that I am not alone in my journey. I would recommend this book for any survivor of sexual abuse to help strengthen their faith and to understand that even when bad things happen to good people, He still has a purpose for each of us."

—Tracy Kelly
http://www.unfilteredtracykelly.com

"A powerful book that educates the reader on childhood sexual abuse, signs, and ways of prevention. One is filled with emotional sorrow for children as this awesome woman shares her life experiences and others from a child, to coping as an adult. The reader learns that sexual childhood abuse is devastating, and leads to years of pain and rejection. You are increased with knowledge and understanding of such a kept secret, and a destroyer of life. The author expresses that a relationship with God is essential, with friends and a support group can lead to freedom, self-acceptance and love. A must-read book."

—Toni Bruce
Precious Stones 4 Life LLC
CEO, Motivational speaker, Best Selling Author
tonib.firstfitness.com

"In reading *Steps of Grace, Ladder of Mercy*, I'm reminded and brought to reality that, Indeed, it is only by God's grace and mercy that will bring us through our story. Let's remember Heb. 13:8 " Jesus Christ is the same yesterday, today, and forever". His **presence** is consistent. His **power** is consistent. What he did 2000 years ago... He can do it today! That's true when it comes to **Saving**.... and **Forgiving**.... and **Restoring**.... and **Redeeming**.... and yes even **Healing.** God's healing touch ... isn't just something of the past....
Steps of Grace, Ladder of Mercy is a powerful message of God's love for His Children whom He created. I recommend adding this book to your reading room."

—Barry Bonner, Senior Pastor

"This book is an inspiration, especially to those of us men and women who have endured abuse! To know that complete healing is real and possible gives a feeling of hope. The deliberate actions Natasha took in believing God's words, walking with Him, and surrendering all of her emotions are remarkable! Natasha shows us that living life the way God intended is a testimony of God's grace!

I learned by reading this book that whatever experiences we have endured are only part of our story. Natasha's book led me to experience God's joy through His love, and longing for all of us to reach out, take hold of His hand and let Him guide us through to a brighter tomorrow. I believe there are better days that await us. What beautiful lessons and stories were shared in this book!

I would recommend this book to all who are looking for inspiration and hope!"

—Deborah Wiener

"Natasha McCoy makes her writing debut with *Steps of Grace, Ladder of Mercy*. The author addresses her childhood sexual trauma history and her healing journey. Her desire to tell her story is motivated in the spirit of helping other adults who have experienced trauma as a child by opening up about her experience. Anyone facing similar history may find this book a worthwhile component to surviving and thriving as they heal from trauma."

—JoEllen Revell, LCSW
Program Director
Victim Service Center of Central Florida

"The trauma of childhood sexual abuse, the courage to fight and the power of one woman to heal."

—Maureen Ryan Blake
Maureen Ryan Blake Media Productions

NOTES

NOTES

NOTES

NOTES

NOTES

NOTES

www.ingramcontent.com/pod-product-compliance
Lightning Source LLC
Chambersburg PA
CBHW060331130626
46553CB00003B/975